It's Going to Be Okay

PAGE PUBLISHING, INC.
Conneaut Lake, PA

First originally published by Page Publishing 2020

ISBN 978-1-64701-653-1 (pbk)
ISBN 978-1-6624-3835-6 (hc)
ISBN 978-1-64701-654-8 (digital)

Printed in the United States of America

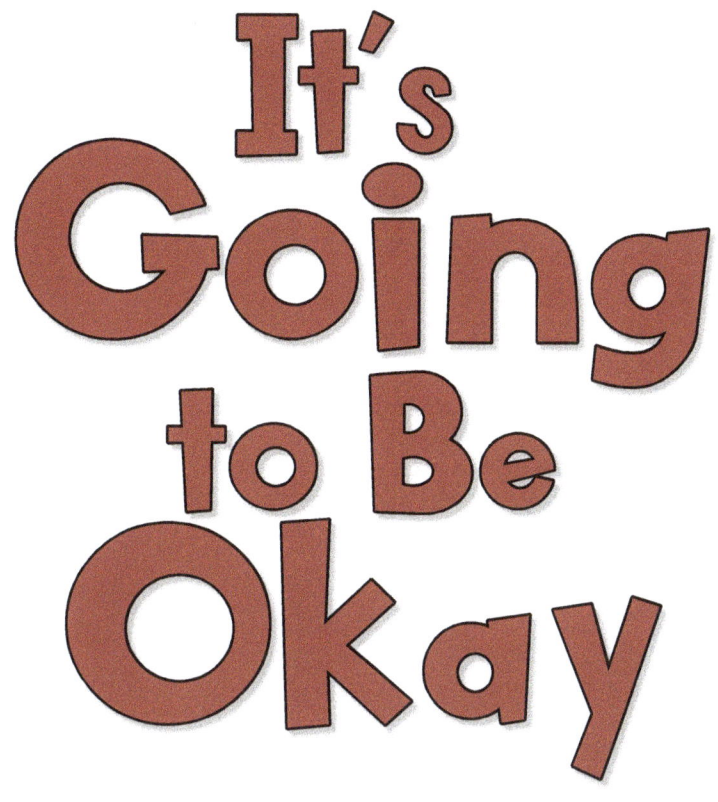

It's Going to Be Okay

MARISSA LORENZANA WALLACE

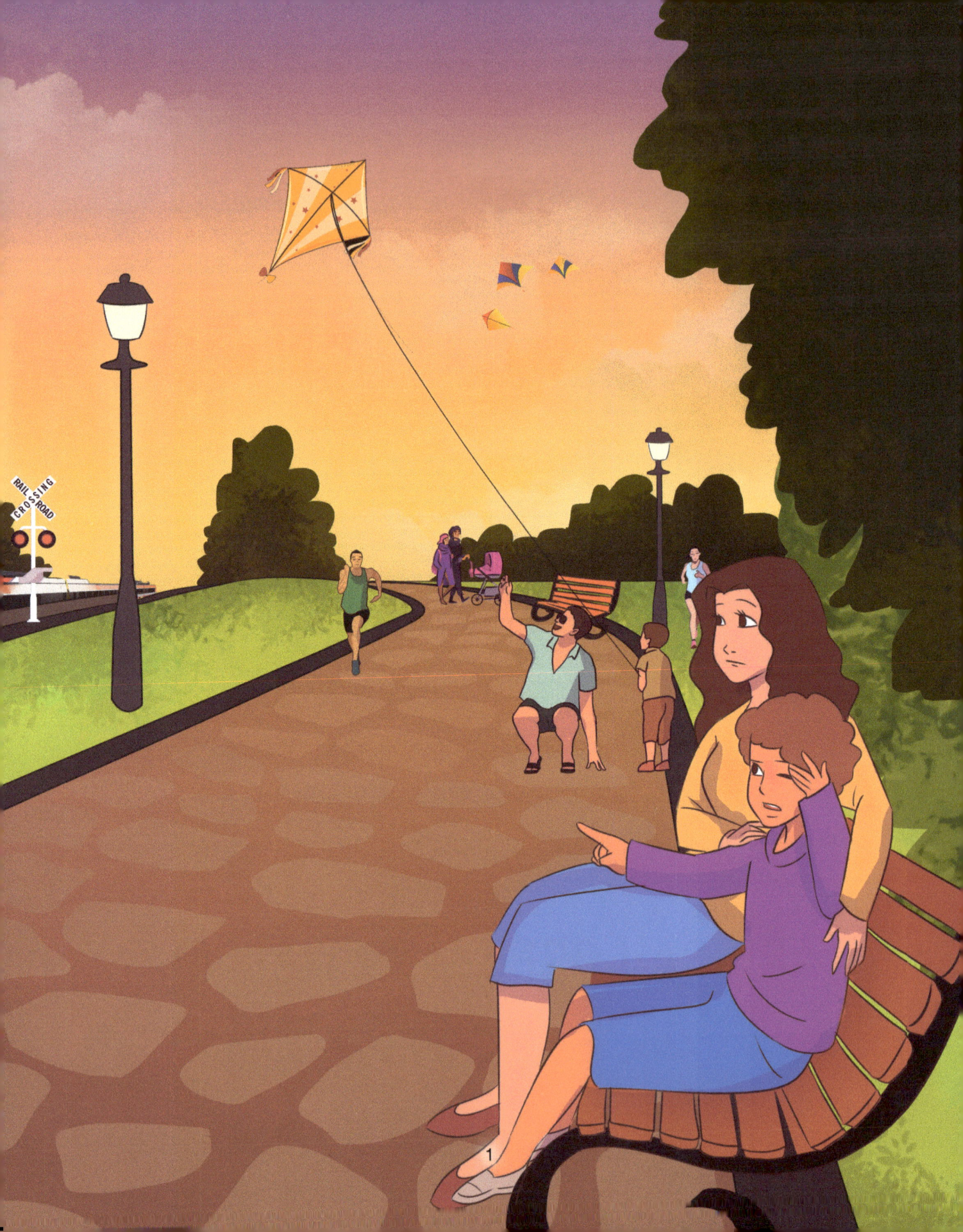

1

"Mommy, it's loud! The train is coming!"

"It's going to be okay. The train blows its horn to let people know to watch out. Let's count the carts."

"Mommy, it's raining! It's loud!"

"It's going to be okay. I've got you. Sometimes the rain is accompanied by thunder and lightning. Thunder is a loud crashing noise heard after lightning flashes."

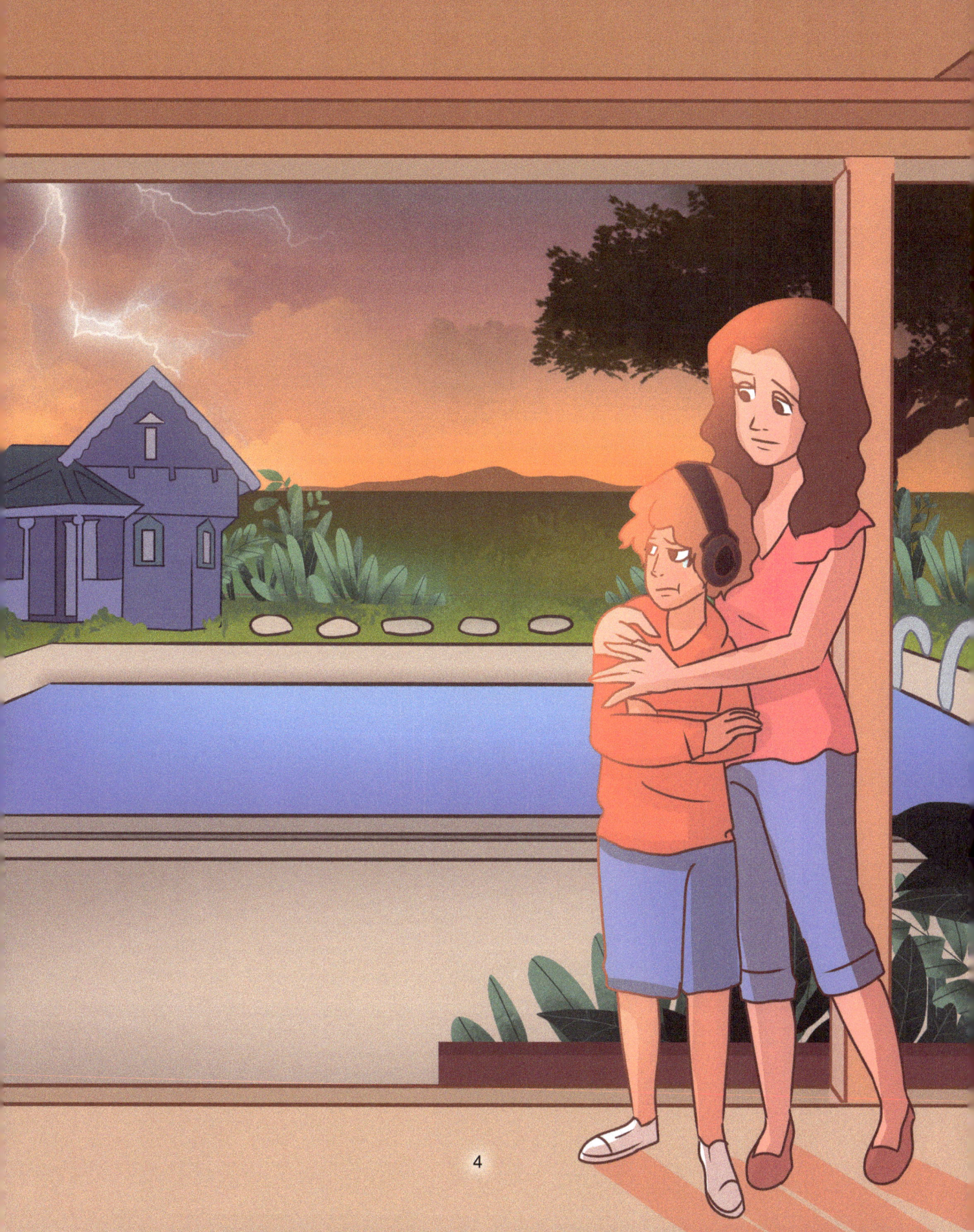

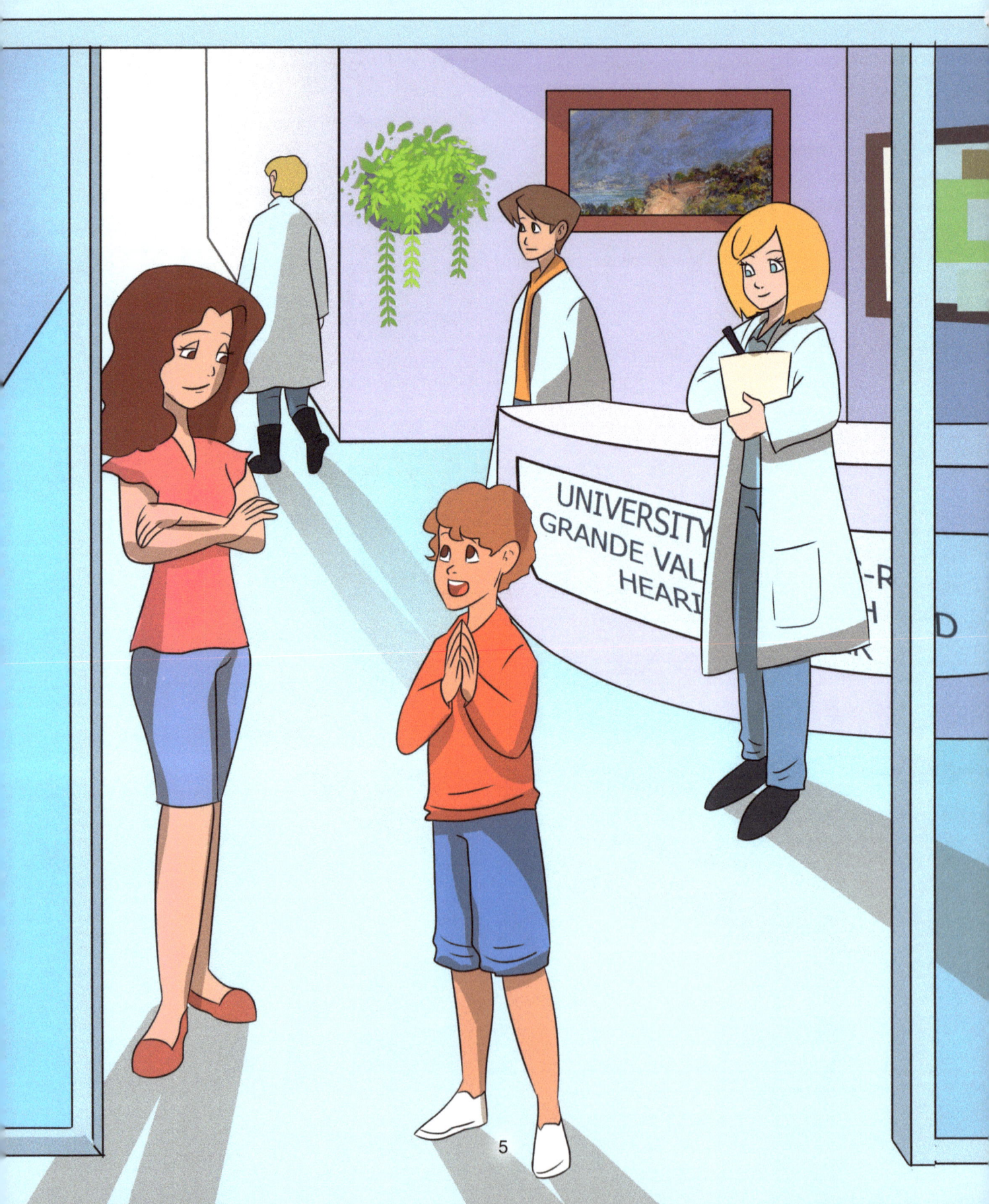

"Mommy, the magic doors!"

"It's going to be okay. Sometimes doors open automatically."

"Mommy, the escalators! Go up and down!"

"It's going to be okay. Sometimes we need to take the escalators to go from one floor to another."

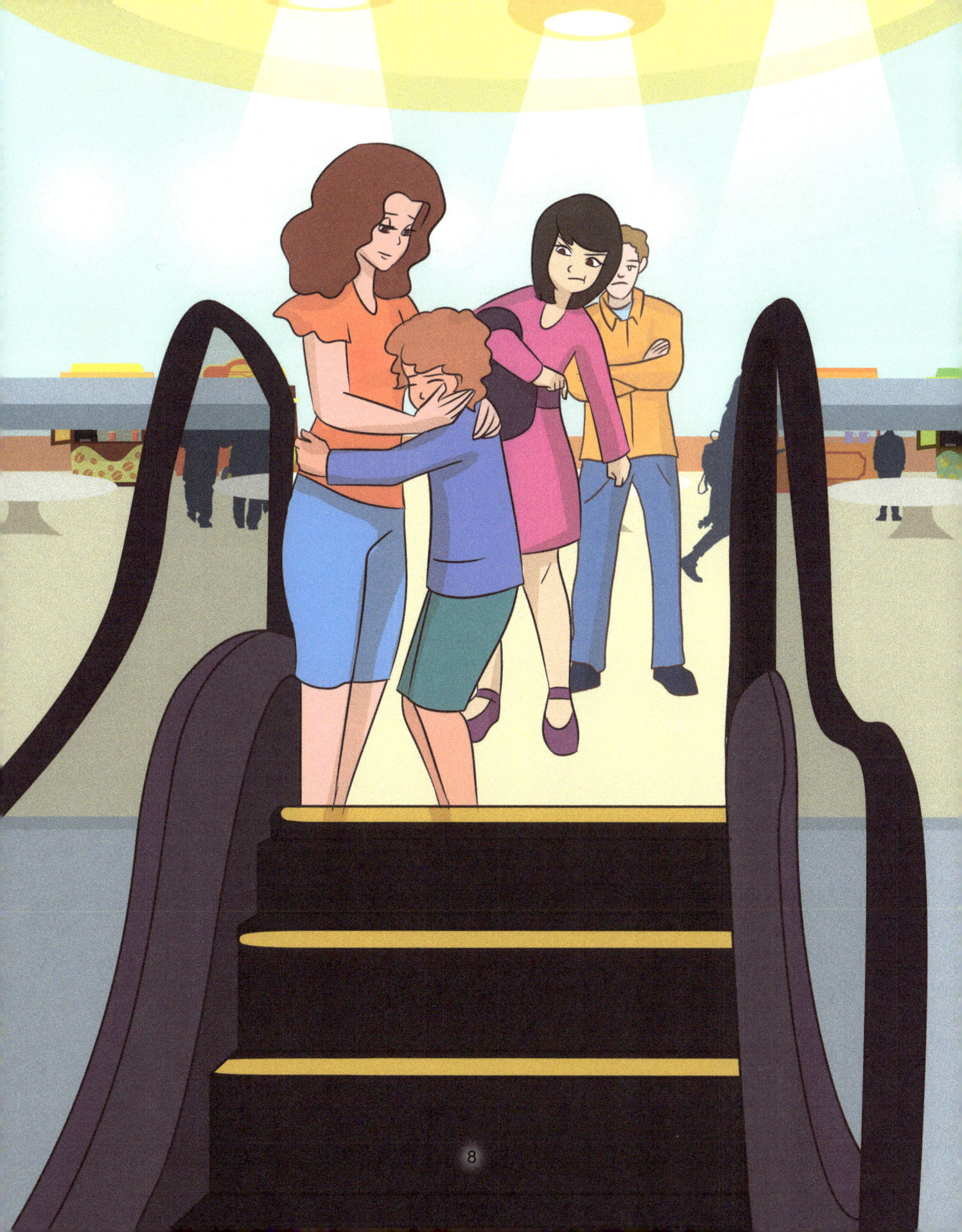

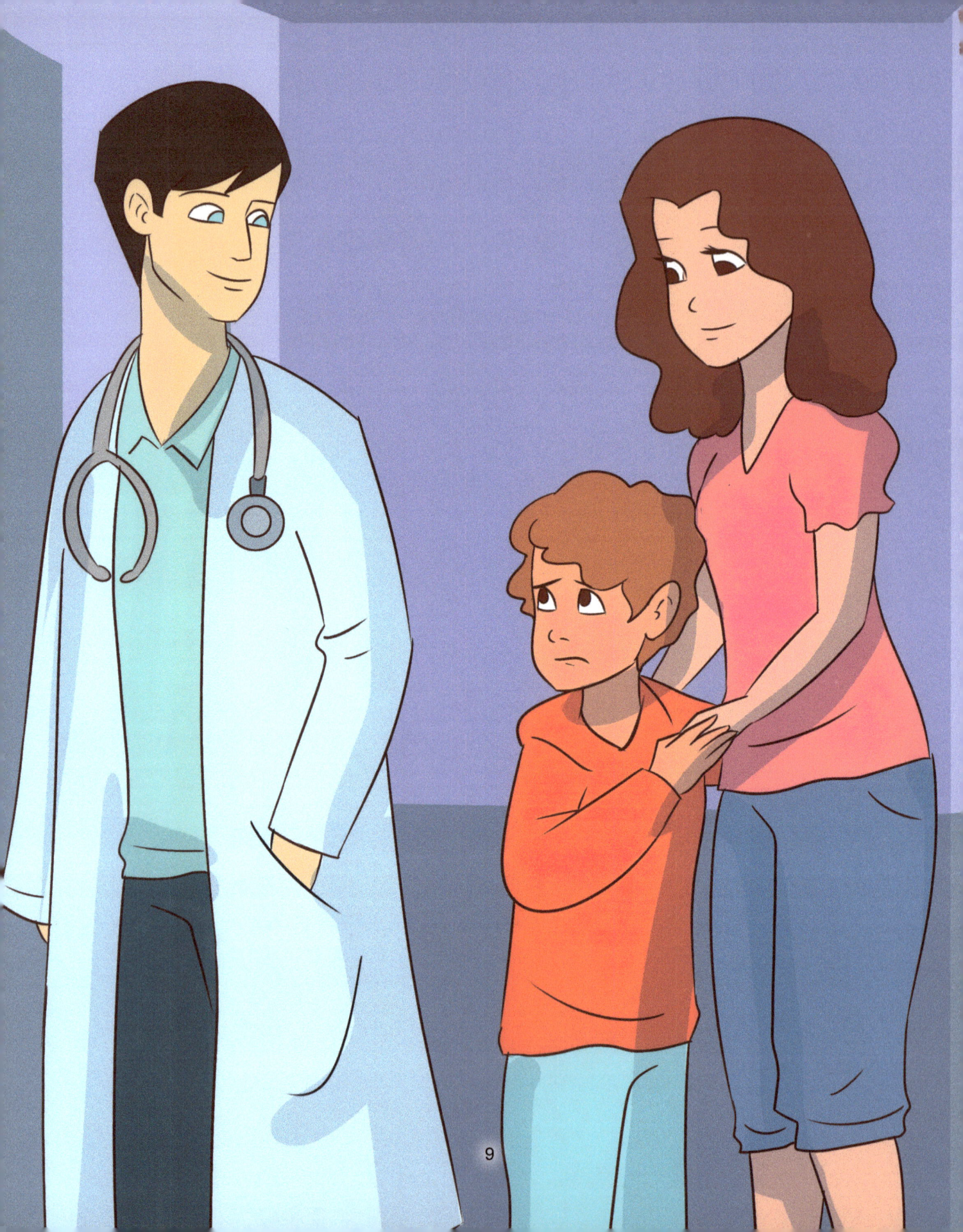

"Mommy, the elevator!"

"It's going to be okay. Press the button. When you press the button, the doors close and the elevator will take you to any floor in the building."

"Mommy, the ceiling fan. Turn on the ceiling fan!"

"It's going to be okay. Sometimes we turn on the ceiling fan when the room gets too hot."

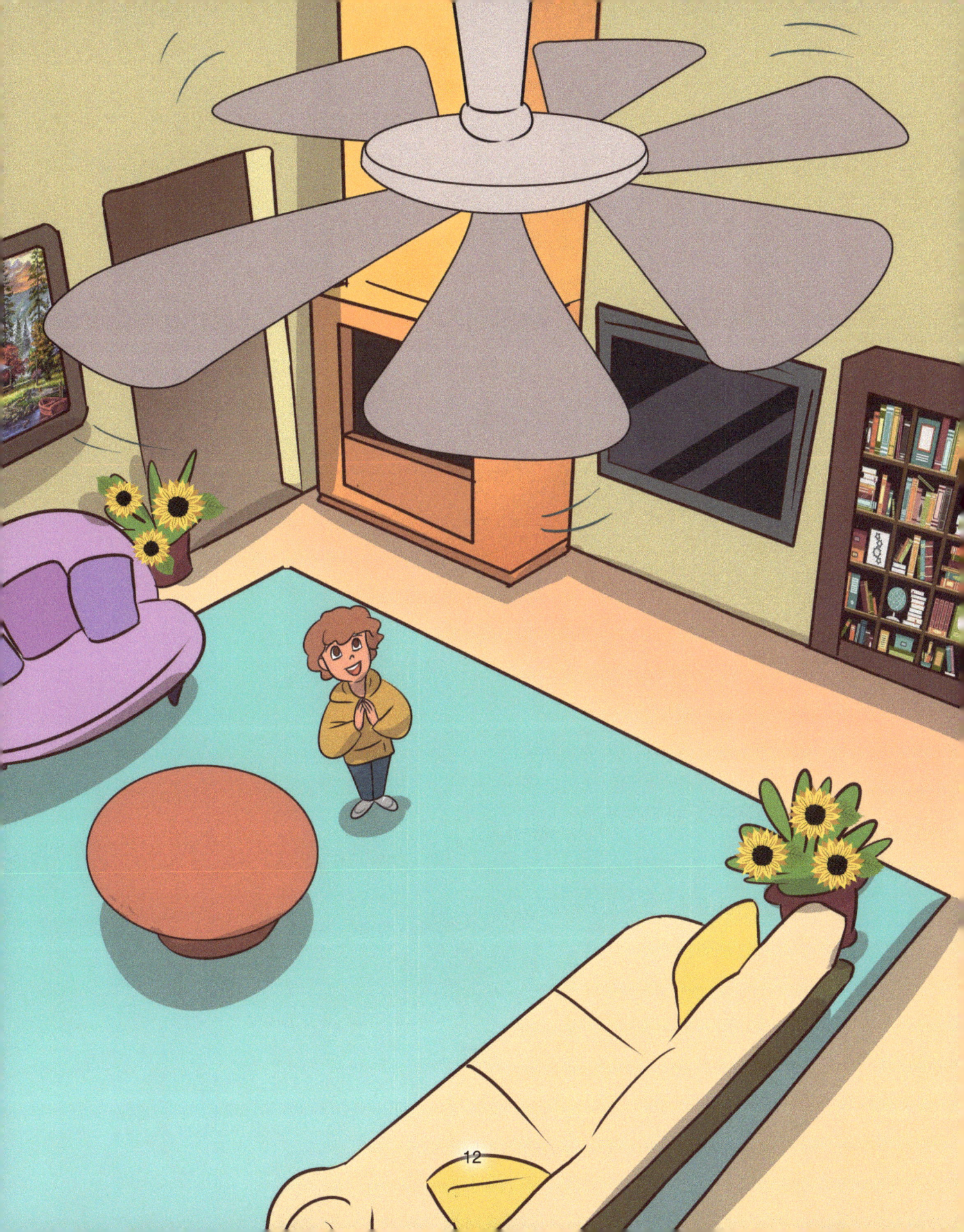

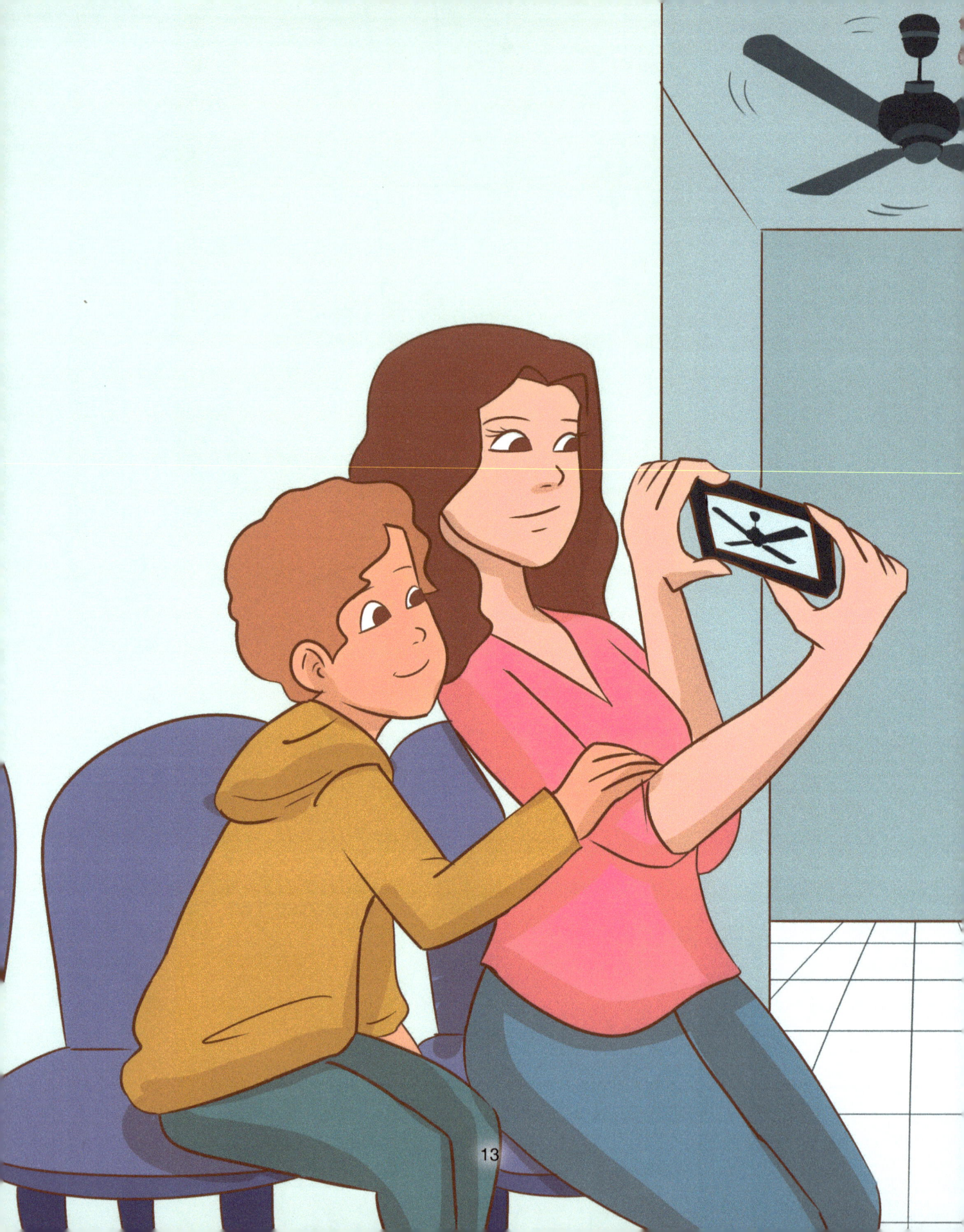

"Mommy, take a video! Take a video!"

"It's going to be okay. I'll take the video."

"Mommy, the oven is beeping!"

"It's going to be okay. That just tells me the oven is ready to bake."

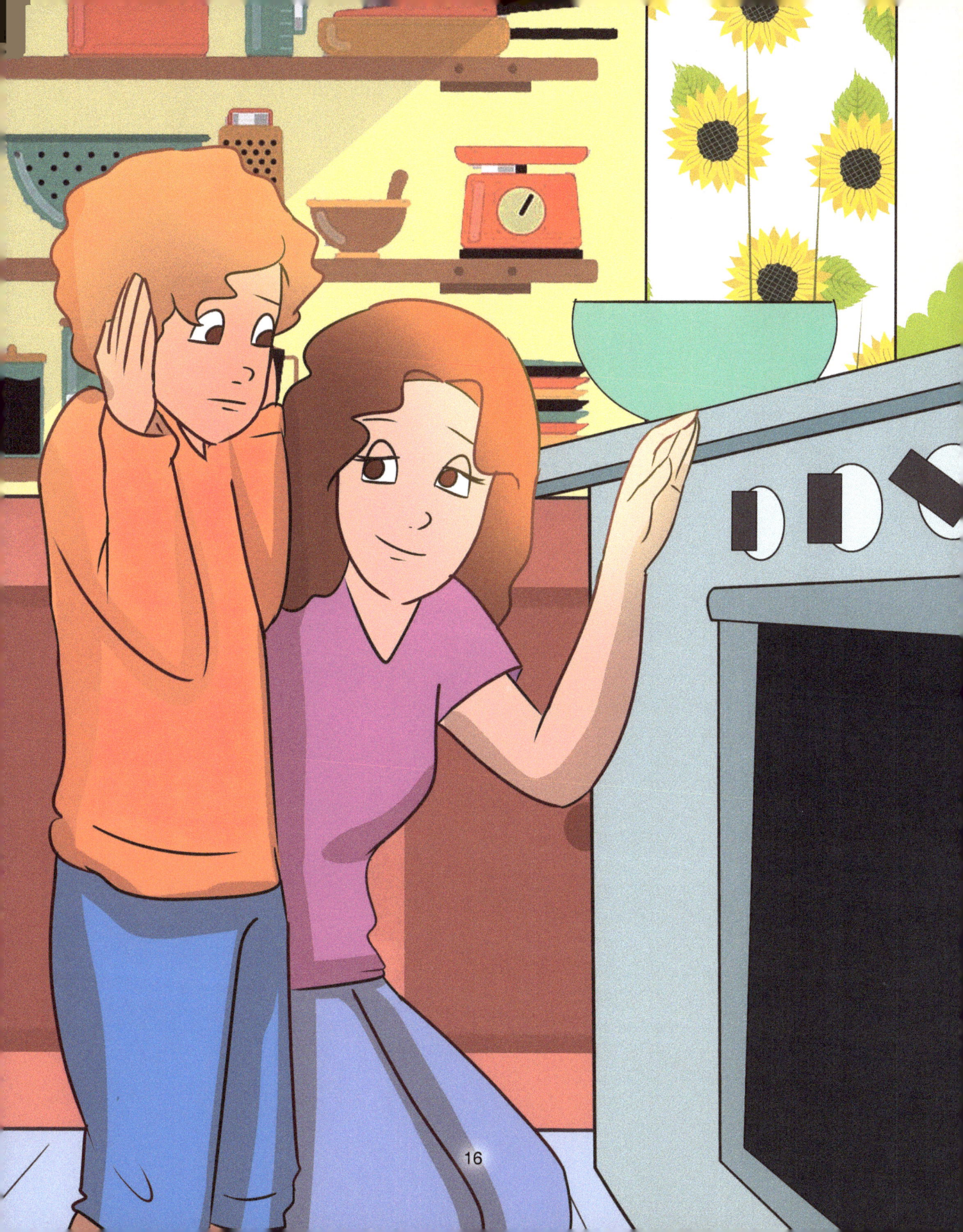
16

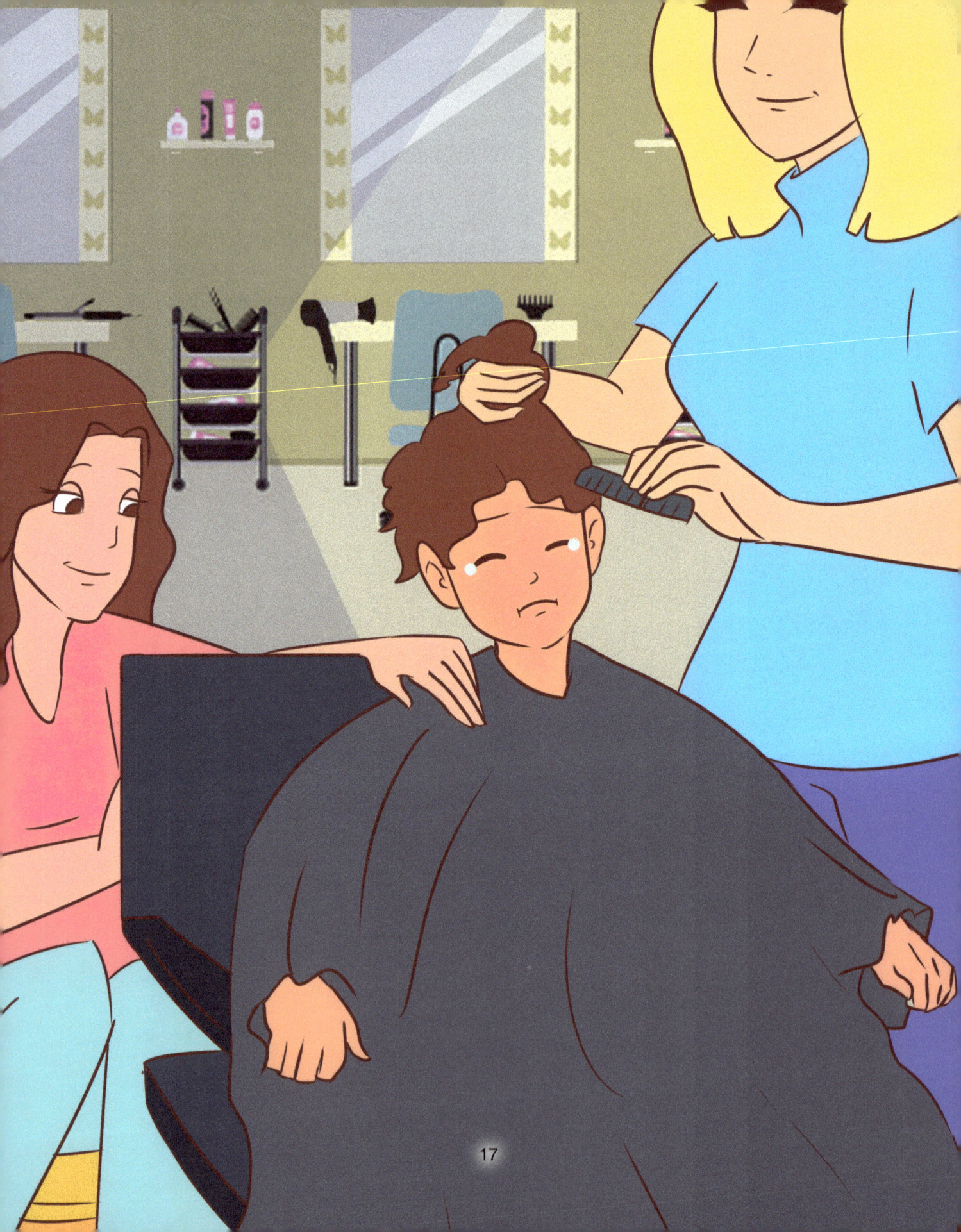

"Mommy, no haircut! The stick is loud!"

"It's going to be okay. The clippers are used to cut and trim hair."

"Mommy, time to cut toenails."

"It's going to be okay. The toenail clippers help keep your nails trim. I'll trim one nail at a time."

"Mommy, my fingernails are getting long."

"It's going to be okay. Just like trimming your toenails, I'll trim your fingernails one at a time. It won't hurt."

"Mommy, my mashed potatoes are hot!"

"It's going to be okay. Blow on them so they can cool down."

"Mommy, the lights are not working!"

"It's going to be okay. Sometimes the lights need to be replaced."

"Mommy, I'm afraid of getting on the train!"

"It's going to be okay. The train ride will take us around the park. It's a lot of fun! Let's put your headphones on."

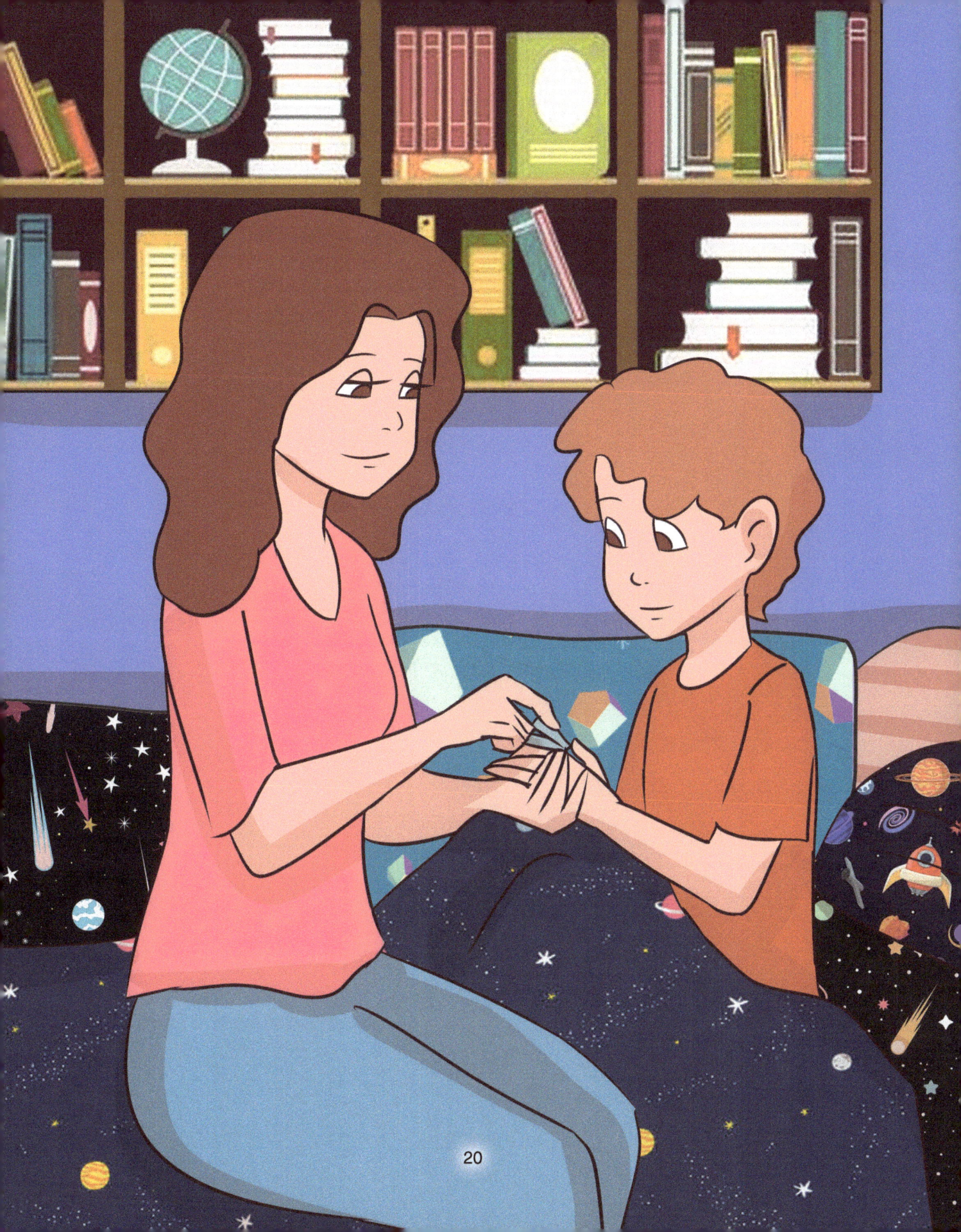

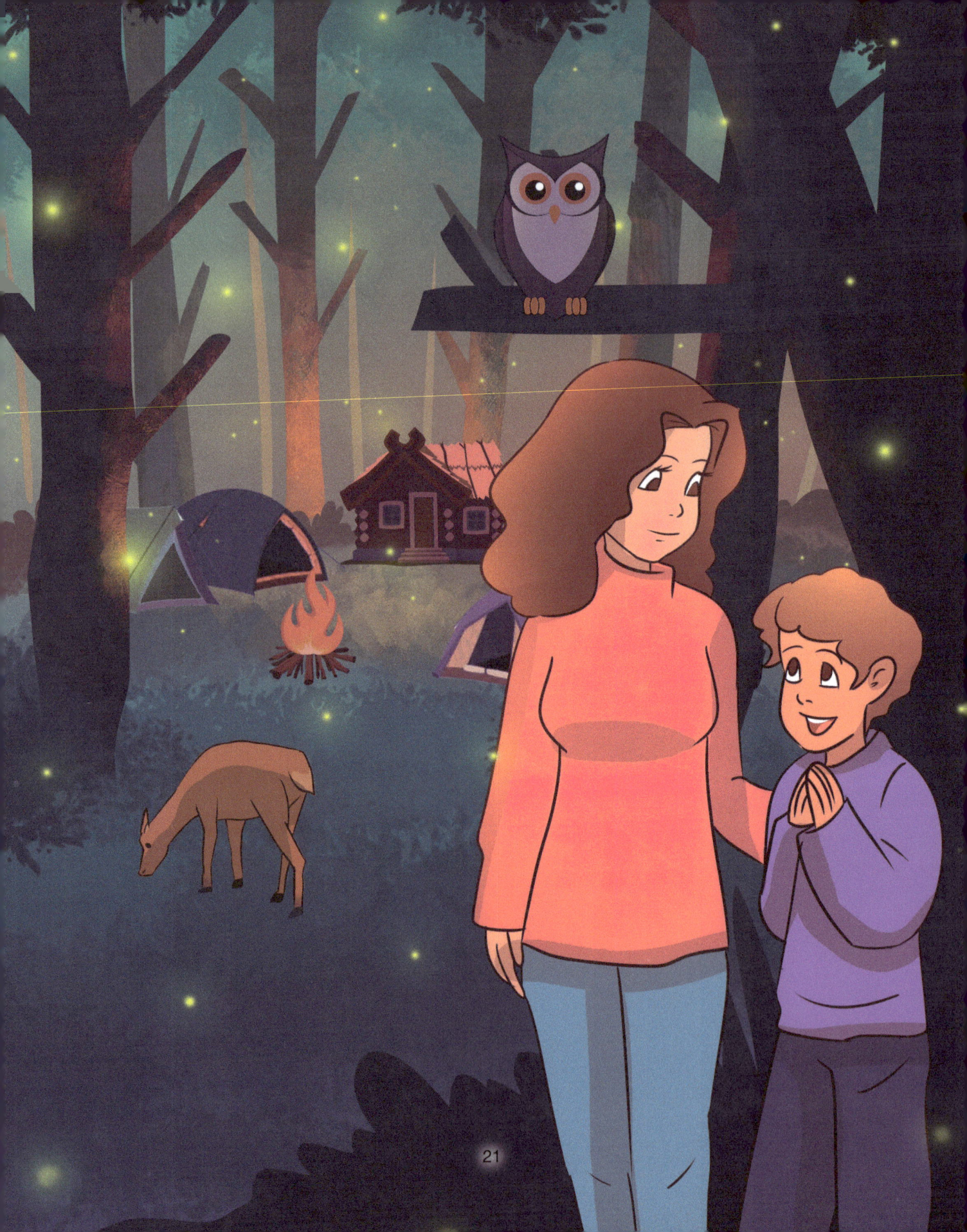

"Mommy, are we going camping and staying in a cabin?"

"It's going to be okay. The cabin is just like Grandma's ranch. There's lots of trees, and when you look up at the night sky, you're going to see bright stars and a full moon."

"Mommy, I see green little lights flying all around the grass."

"It's going to be okay. Those are fireflies. Remember that Grandma's ranch is full of fireflies. They light up and sparkle at night."

"Mommy, I want to hear the song. Play it again."

"It's going to be okay. The song is going to repeat itself over and over again. I love the way you sing."

"Mommy, it's time to go to bed and read a book."

"It's going to be okay. Let's read a story, and then I'll turn off the lights. Good night, my brave little boy."

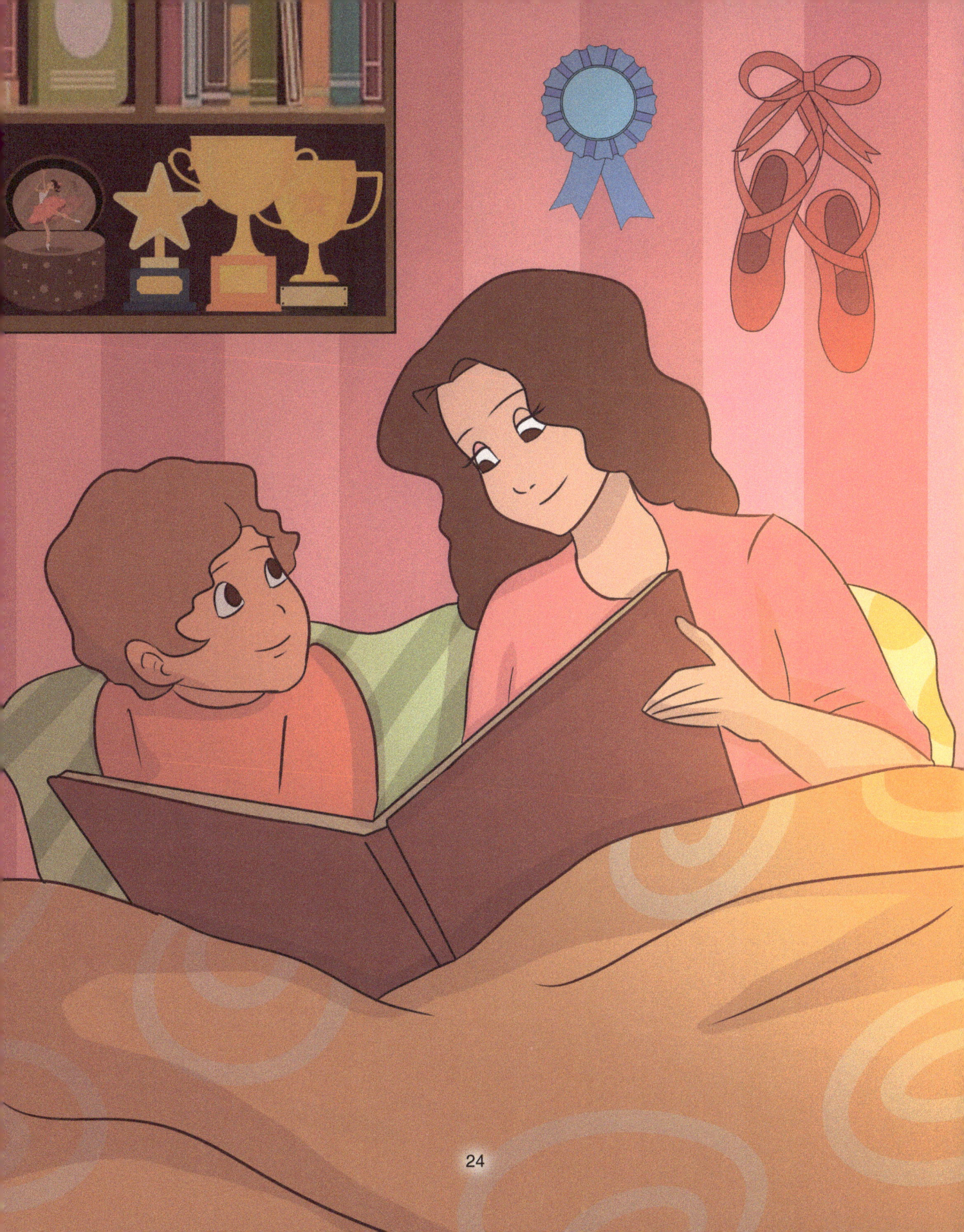

24

About the Author

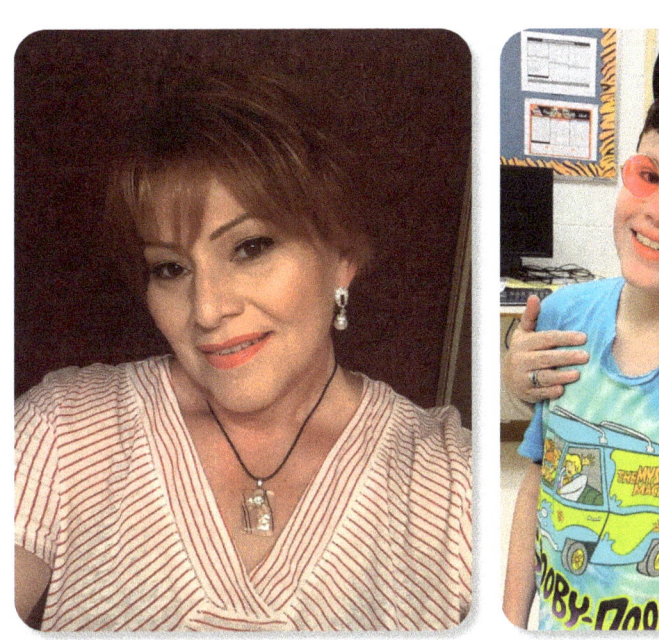 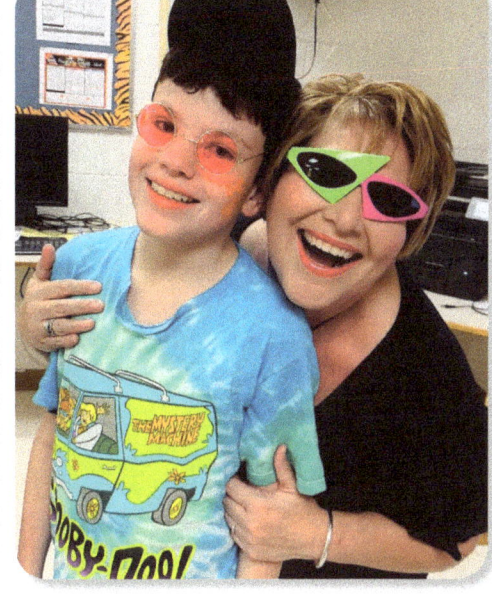

Marissa Lorenzana Wallace was born in Edinburg, Texas, in the Rio Grande Valley. She is a graduate of Mercedes High School (1987) and a graduate of the University of North Texas. Her inspirations are her father, who passed away on February 15, 2018; her mother, who was a Spanish and English teacher for thirty years; her son, Ethan John Wallace, who is autistic; her husband of eighteen years, John Craig Wallace

III; and all her former students and children struggling with a disability, like autism.

She is the middle child of her family and has one older brother and one younger sister.

She lives in Mercedes, Texas, with her family and is often found at her parents' ranch outside of Mercedes.

She is constantly surrounded by family and friends, who never lost faith in her work as a musician, artist, and now author.

She loves traveling, seeking new adventures with her son and husband, camping, horseback riding, making glass sculptures and jewelry, ceramics, walking around her hometown, riding her bike, singing, reading, and most of all, writing.

She is an advocate for special needs children and for the arts.